GREAT MOMENTS IN AMERICAN HISTORY

Gunfight at the O.K. Corral

Wyatt Earp Upholds the Law

Scott Waldman

rosen central
Primary Source™

The Rosen Publishing Group, Inc., New York

Published in 2004 by The Rosen Publishing Group, Inc.
29 East 21st Street, New York, NY 10010

Editor: Eric Fein
Book Design: Erica Clendening
Photo researcher: Rebecca Anguin-Cohen
Series photo researcher: Jeff Wendt

Photo Credits: Cover (left), title page, p. 18 © Bowers Museum of Cultural Art/Corbis; cover (right)
illustration © Debra Wainwright/The Rosen Publishing Group; pp. 6, 14, 22 courtesy Arizona Historical
Society/Tucson; p. 10 Camilius S. Fly, © Collection of the New York Historical Society NYHS# 40746;
p. 29 courtesy of the Autry Museum of Western Heritage, Los Angeles; p. 30 Western History Collections,
University of Oklahoma Libraries; p. 31 © Christie's Images/Corbis; p. 32 courtesy Tombstone Epitaph,
Tombstone, AZ, 85638

First Edition

Publisher Cataloging Data

Waldman, Scott P.
    Gunfight at the O.K. Corral: Wyatt Earp upholds the law / by Scott Waldman.
    p. cm.—(Great moments in American history)
    Summary: Wyatt, Virgil, and Morgan Earp, along with Doc Holliday, defend
    themselves against the McLaurys and the Clantons in 1881.
    ISBN 0-8239-4393-3 (lib. bdg.)
    1. Earp, Wyatt, 1848-1929—Juvenile literature 2. Tombstone (Ariz.) History—19th
    century—Juvenile literature 3. Clanton family—Juvenile literature 4. Earp
    family—Juvenile literature 5. Peace officers—Arizona—Tombstone—Biography—
    Juvenile literature 6. Outlaws—Arizona—Tombstone—Biography—Juvenile
    literature 7. Violence—Arizona—Tombstone—History—19th century—Juvenile
    literature   8. Frontier and pioneer life—Arizona—Tombstone—Juvenile literature
    9. Tombstone (Ariz.)—Biography—Juvenile literature [1. Earp, Wyatt, 1848-1929
    2. Tombstone (Ariz.)—History 3. Violence 4. Robbers and outlaws 5. Frontier
    and pioneer life—Arizona— Tombstone] I. Title   II. Series

    F819.T6 W195 2004
    979.1'53—dc21   2003-009732

CONTENTS

Preface

The American West during the 1800s was a growing—yet dangerous—time and place. The discovery of gold and silver brought many people West. People from all across America and from many parts of the world came to find their fortunes in the West. Most of these people were hardworking. Many, however, were criminals. They robbed and often killed other people. Crimes such as cattle rustling, or stealing cattle, also became very common.

Most people lived by the code of the West. The code was a set of unwritten and unspoken rules about how people should act. The main idea of the code was that people should honor, respect, and work with their neighbors. Even with this understanding between people, crime was almost everywhere. Often, disagreements were settled by violence.

Wyatt Earp was born on March 19, 1848, in Monmouth, Illinois. As a young man, Earp worked many different jobs. He was a buffalo hunter, a stagecoach driver, and a peace officer. In 1876, he became a deputy marshal in Dodge City, Kansas. Earp moved to the town of Tombstone, Arizona in 1879, where he became a deputy sheriff.

The town of Tombstone had been built near a large silver mine. It attracted many people hoping to strike it rich. By 1880, about six thousand people lived in Tombstone. However, there were not enough jobs in town to support that many people. Silver was also becoming harder to find. Some people turned to crime to support themselves. Some began stealing cattle. The stealing of cattle in Tombstone would lead to one of the most dramatic events in the Old West. It would also change the life of Wyatt Earp forever. . . .

Wyatt Earp (above) was born on March 19, 1848, in Monmouth, Illinois. Earp's father, Nicholas, served in an army unit during the Mexican-American War. He named his son in honor of his commanding officer, Wyatt Berry Stapp.

Chapter One

Trouble Brewing

On a hot day in July 1880, Wyatt Earp and his brothers, Virgil and Morgan, rode out to the McLaury ranch. The McLaurys were known cattle rustlers and they were dangerous people. The Earps were going there to look into the stealing of six mules from a nearby U.S. Army base, Camp Rucker.

"You think there's going to be trouble?" Morgan asked. He wiped the sweat from his forehead with the back of his hand.

"Of course. You don't think that they'll just admit to stealing, do you?" Virgil said. Virgil was the city marshal for Tombstone. He was responsible for dealing with crime inside the city. However, he found himself dealing with crimes outside of

Tombstone because the sheriff, John Behan, refused to crack down on rustlers.

"If they want trouble, they'll get trouble," Wyatt said. To make his point, he patted the revolver at his side.

"Easy, Wyatt," Virgil said. "You and Morgan are my deputies. You follow my lead."

The Earps were not welcomed at the McLaury ranch. However, that didn't stop them from doing their job. They searched the ranch. While they did not find the stolen mules, they did find evidence that the McLaurys were involved in the theft.

"I want those mules turned over to us right now," Virgil said to Tom McLaury.

"That's not possible at the moment," said McLaury. "But, I promise, I'll return them as soon as I can."

Virgil looked at Wyatt, who shrugged. The Earps didn't have much choice. They were outnumbered by the McLaury family and their workers. The Earps knew this was no time to start a fight with the McLaurys.

"They're not going to give back those mules," Wyatt said, as the Earps rode back to Tombstone.

"I know," Virgil said. "But if I were to try to arrest them, they'd get their politician friends, like Sheriff John Behan, to get them out of trouble. We'll get our chance at them someday."

Over the next several months, tensions between the Earps and the McLaurys got worse. Friends of the McLaurys, the Clanton family, also did not like the Earps. The Clantons were cattle rustlers and did business with the McLaurys. On many occasions, the Clantons and the McLaurys threatened to kill the Earps. The Earps continued to try to enforce the law the best they could. However, everyone knew that the feud would end only one way—with spilled blood.

Ike Clanton's full name was Joseph Isaac Clanton. He was born in Missouri, in 1847. This is the only known picture of him.

Chapter Two

Ike Clanton Goes Wild

As the months went on, things got worse for the Earps. The McLaurys and the Clantons spread untrue stories about the Earps. The townspeople began to distrust the Earps. However, Wyatt had one major advantage in any fight. He had Doc Holliday on his side. People called him 'Doc' because he was a dentist. He was very quick with his guns.

Doc Holliday never backed down from a fight. He was dying from a lung illness called tuberculosis. Because he knew he was dying, Holliday had no fear in a gunfight. He was also an excellent card player. He won a lot of money from the rustlers. This fact, and because he was a friend of the Earps, made him an enemy of the McLaurys and the Clantons.

On the night of October 25, 1881, Ike Clanton got drunk. On the streets of Tombstone, he exclaimed that he was going to kill the Earps. Doc Holliday found Clanton and challenged him to a gunfight on the spot. Since Tombstone had a law against carrying guns in town, Clanton didn't have a gun on him.

"If I had a gun, I'd shoot you right now!" Clanton said.

"If you had a gun right now, you'd be dead," Holliday replied, smiling. He turned to face the crowd. "If anyone here has a gun, please give it to Ike so we can settle this right now."

Fortunately for Clanton, no one had a gun. Just then, the Earp brothers showed up. Morgan Earp broke up the fight. Clanton looked Wyatt right in the eye.

"Tomorrow, I want to fight you, man to man," Clanton said.

"You know where to find me," Wyatt replied as he turned away. He kept his hand on his gun.

Clanton spent the rest of the night gambling and drinking. The next morning, he got a shotgun and went walking through town. He was yelling that he was going to shoot the first Earp he saw. Virgil heard what was going on. He hid behind a corner of a nearby building. When Clanton walked by, Virgil jumped out behind him. Just as Clanton turned around to face him, Virgil hit him hard across the head with the butt of his gun. Clanton fell to the ground. Virgil had knocked out Clanton. Clanton had a cut on his forehead.

Virgil took Clanton to court for carrying a shotgun in the town. The judge fined Clanton twenty-five dollars and let him go. By then, Wyatt and Tom McLaury both had heard what had happened. They rushed to the courthouse to hear what the judge would say. As the men were leaving, Wyatt and Tom got in a fight. It ended when Wyatt hit McLaury with his gun. McLaury ran off, holding his head. He vowed that all of the Earp brothers would pay for what they had done.

This photo of Tombstone, Arizona was taken in 1881. Tombstone was founded by Ed Schieffelin after he discovered silver in the area.

The Long Walk

On the afternoon of October 26, the McLaurys and Clantons went to the O.K. Corral. They were keeping their horses at the corral while they were in town. They were going to ride back to their ranch outside of town. There, they would come up with a plan to deal with the Earps and Doc Holliday. Ike Clanton, however, could not be calmed down enough to leave.

"I'll make those Earps pay for embarrassing me!" he shouted. "If they were here right now, they'd all get a bullet from my gun to chew on!"

"Why are we running away like chickens?" Billy Clanton asked. "Let's go get them right now. Give me a chance with that Doc Holliday. I'll show him who's quick with a gun!"

A young boy whose father was a friend of the Earps heard the Clantons and McLaurys talking. He ran through the town until he found Virgil Earp.

"The Clanton and McLaury rustlers are saying that they're gonna get you guys before they leave town," he said.

"Thanks for letting me know," Virgil said. He went to get Morgan and Wyatt.

"We have work to do," he said to his brothers. "The Clantons and McLaurys are down at the O.K. Corral, threatening our lives. We need to go get their guns and put a stop to this."

"They're the ones who are going to get hurt," Wyatt said. He picked up his Colt revolver from the table. Wyatt only used his gun whenever he had to. If there was a way to avoid having to use his gun, Wyatt would do so. He knew that the Clantons and McLaurys would not stop until someone was dead. Wyatt was going to make sure that it wasn't him or any of his brothers.

"I told them if they wanted a fight, I'd give them one," he said.

The three men started for the O.K. Corral. On their way, they met Doc Holliday. "What's going on?" Holliday asked.

"Nothing," Wyatt said. "Go back to your gambling."

"You're going to face off against the Clantons and the McLaurys," Holliday said.

"It's none of your business, Doc," Wyatt said. This got Holliday mad. "Don't you tell me this ain't my business. We're friends. And friends stick together, no matter what the danger."

Wyatt sighed. "Fine, you crazy old dentist. Get yourself shot. See if I care."

Holliday smiled. Virgil made Holliday a deputy and handed him a large shotgun. Holliday hid it underneath his long coat. Then the four men headed down the street for the O.K. Corral—and history!

Victor Clyde Forsythe painted *Fight at the O.K. Corral*. Forsythe was a famous painter of the Old West. He often lived in ghost towns while on his painting trips.

Chapter Four

Shoot-out!

Sheriff Behan ran up to the Earps and asked them to stop.

"You know we can't do that, sheriff," Wyatt said. "Those boys are dangerous."

"If you want to help us enforce the law, come along," Virgil offered. "Otherwise, stand aside."

Behan turned and ran towards the O.K. Corral. Slowly, the Earp brothers and Doc Holliday walked in the same direction. Each man had his hand on his gun. Townspeople peeked out from their windows. When the group turned the last corner before the corral, five men stared them down. Ike and Billy Clanton were there, as well as Tom and Frank McLaury, and Billy Claiborne. Claiborne was a friend of the rustlers.

Again, Sheriff Behan came up to the Earps and asked them to stop. The rustlers turned around and walked away as he did this. Wyatt told Behan to get out of the way. Behan ran and hid behind a barrel. The Earps and Holliday followed the group of rustlers. The rustlers stopped in a nearby empty lot. They turned to face the Earps and Holliday. The two groups of men stood only ten feet apart.

"Throw up your hands!" Virgil yelled.

Billy Claiborne and Ike Clanton ran away. Both sides yelled things out at each other. Suddenly, there was a click. Wyatt knew that sound: It was the sound of a gun about to be fired. Wyatt whipped out his gun and aimed it at Frank McLaury. Frank was the quickest shot of all the rustlers. Just as Wyatt aimed, a shot rang out from one of the rustlers.

Bullets and gunsmoke filled the air. Frank McLaury had been hit in the stomach. Ike Clanton ran back to the fight. He grabbed Wyatt's arm, yelling at him to stop. Since Ike did not have a gun, Wyatt just pushed him away.

Again, Ike ran off. Virgil Earp was then hit in the leg with a bullet. Though hurt, Frank McLaury and Billy Clanton, who was also shot, were still firing wildly. Tom McLaury hid behind his horse and shot Morgan.

"Wyatt, I've been hit!" yelled Morgan, holding his shoulder.

"Get down!" Wyatt yelled at his brother as he aimed for Tom McLaury. He hit Tom's horse, and it took off. Doc Holliday blew Tom McLaury off his feet with a shotgun blast. He then threw down the shotgun and got out his revolver. Morgan tripped and fell. He looked up to see Frank McLaury and Holliday pointing their guns at one another. He aimed for Frank's head and squeezed the trigger. At the same moment, Frank fired at Holliday, but the bullet only skimmed off his hip. Frank tumbled over, dead. With that, the gun battle was finished. It had only lasted thirty seconds. Tom and Frank McLaury, and Billy Clanton lay dead. Virgil, Morgan, and Holliday all had been shot. Wyatt remained unhurt.

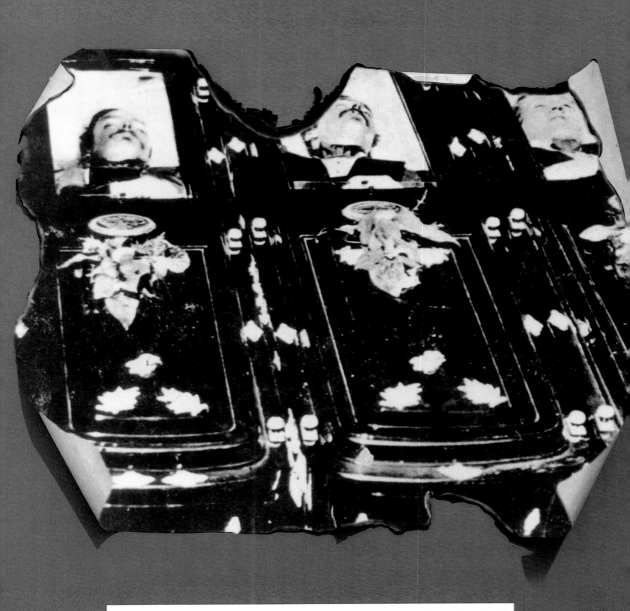

The O.K. Corral gunfight left three men dead. The dead men are, from left to right, Tom McLaury, Frank McLaury, and Billy Clanton.

22

Chapter Five

Lawmen or Killers?

When the shooting had stopped, Sheriff Behan came out from where he had been hiding. He headed straight for the Earps. "You boys are under arrest for murder!" he cried.

"Go home, sheriff," Wyatt said. "We were just doing our job. You won't be making any arrests today."

Wyatt got medical help for his brothers and Holliday. The bodies of Billy Clanton and Tom and Frank McLaury were taken to the undertaker. The funeral for the McLaurys and Billy Clanton was the largest ever held in Tombstone.

A few days after the shoot-out, the official investigation into the events at the O.K. Corral began. Ike Clanton asked that murder charges be filed against the Earps and Holliday. Because of this, Virgil was suspended from his marshal job.

The Earps were put on trial. The trial went on for a month. Many people were called as witnesses. Each person told a different version of the shoot-out.

"It was all the Earps' doing," Ike Clanton said. "We weren't doing anything wrong. None of us even had guns. Virgil and the others came up to us out of the blue and told us to raise our hands. He said we were under arrest. Before we could reach for the sky, the Earps and their buddy Doc Holliday started blasting away at us!"

Clanton stopped talking and wiped his face with his handkerchief, then blew his nose with it. "I'm sorry, your honor. Pardon me," he said. "It's hard seeing your brother and your friends murdered."

"It's all right," the judge said. "Take all the time you want."

Wyatt and Holliday sat in the courtroom listening to Ike Clanton speak. Wyatt was angry. He made his hands into fists and pounded them against his thighs. "He's lying out of both sides

of his mouth," Wyatt said to Holliday.

"Easy, Wyatt. You'll get your chance to tell your side of the story," Holliday said.

More people spoke out in court against the Earps and Holliday. Finally, Wyatt got his chance to tell his side of the story. He took the stand and promised to tell the truth. "We weren't out to kill anyone," he began. "We were just trying to settle our feud with the Clantons and the McLaurys. It had been getting worse for the last year or so.

"Then, the night before the shoot-out, Ike Clanton went around town promising to kill me and my brothers. We tried to look the other way, but Clanton and his friends left us with no choice. The very next day, he was at it again. We knew we had to do something before an innocent person got hurt."

Wyatt was asked why he started shooting. He said it was because he heard the sound of the hammer of a gun being pulled back.

The judge listened to everyone's stories. He carefully thought about who was responsible for the shooting. He ruled that the Earps and Holliday were *not* guilty of murder. They had done the right thing by protecting themselves. Many people were unhappy with the decision. Most of them were friends of the Clantons and McLaurys.

The courtroom exploded in yelling and shouts. Wyatt felt relief. He shook hands with Holliday. Outside, some of their friends met them to congratulate them on winning.

"You did it, Wyatt. You're in the clear. Your troubles are over," said one of Wyatt's friends.

Wyatt smiled sadly and shook his head. "No," he said. "I have a bad feeling that the feud between me and the Clantons isn't over. Not by a long shot."

He was right. There was more pain and death down the road for him and his brothers. But *that* is a story for another time.

Glossary

arrest (uh-REST) to stop and hold someone by the power of law

corral (kuh-RAL) a fenced area that holds horses, cattle, or other animals

dangerous (DAYN-jur-uhss) likely to cause harm or injury

enforce (en-FORSS) to make sure that a law or rule is obeyed

feud (FYOOD) a bitter quarrel between two people, families, or groups that lasts for a long time

investigation (in-VESS-tuh-gay-shuhn) the act of finding out as much as possible about an event, such as a crime

revolver (ri-VOL-vur) a small firearm that stores bullets in a cylinder and can fire several shots before it needs to be loaded again

rustlers (RUHSS-uh-luhrs) people who steal horses or cattle

suspended (suh-SPEND-dhed) being stopped from doing something for a period of time

threatened (THRET-uhned) put in danger

trial (TRYE-uhl) the examination of evidence in a court of law to decide if a charge or claim is true

undertaker (UHN-dur-tay-kur) someone whose job is to arrange funerals and prepare dead bodies to be buried or cremated

Primary Sources

To learn about the people, places, and events of long ago we can study sources such as old letters, diaries, photos, and drawings. These kinds of sources allow us to understand how and why things happened. The drawing shown on page 29 was done with the help of Wyatt Earp. It was made several years after the gunfight at the O.K. Corral and shows how he remembers the event taking place. We can use this drawing to compare and contrast Earp's version of events to other people's accounts of the shoot-out.

The newspaper article shown on page 32 helps us analyze how the law system worked in the Old West in the 1880s. We can see how much money Earp had to pay to stay out of jail during his trial. The drawing and the newspaper article help us understand some of the many details of this famous day in American history.

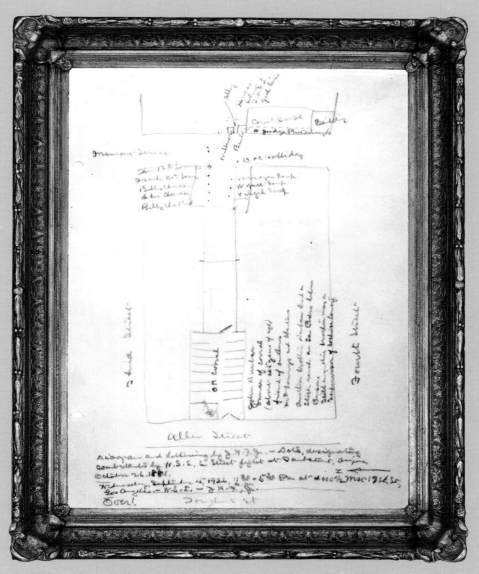

Wyatt Earp helped draw this picture in 1926, three years before he died. The drawing shows where Earp remembered all the gunmen at the O.K. Corral were at the time of the shootings. The drawing was used in the book *Wyatt Earp, Frontier Marshall* written by Stuart Lake.

This photo of Doc Holliday was taken in the early 1880s. Holliday's full name was John Henry Holliday. He grew up in Georgia and studied dentistry in Pennsylvania in the early 1870s.

Cattle rustlers were hard to catch because cattle were often not branded, or marked, by their owners. When branding became more common, rustlers found ways to change the brands put on the cattle.

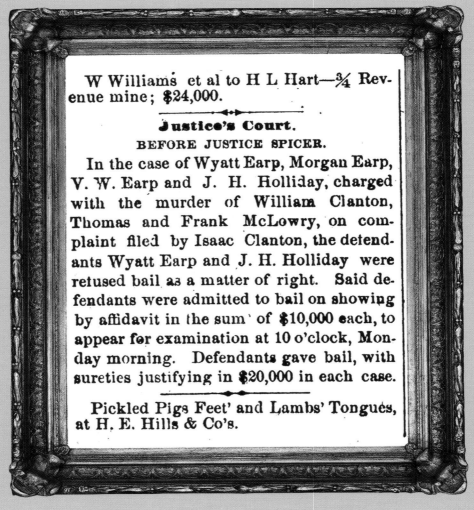

W Williams et al to H L Hart—¾ Revenue mine; $24,000.

Justice's Court.

BEFORE JUSTICE SPICER.

In the case of Wyatt Earp, Morgan Earp, V. W. Earp and J. H. Holliday, charged with the murder of William Clanton, Thomas and Frank McLowry, on complaint filed by Isaac Clanton, the defendants Wyatt Earp and J. H. Holliday were refused bail as a matter of right. Said defendants were admitted to bail on showing by affidavit in the sum of $10,000 each, to appear for examination at 10 o'clock, Monday morning. Defendants gave bail, with sureties justifying in $20,000 in each case.

Pickled Pigs Feet' and Lambs' Tongues, at H. E. Hills & Co's.

This article was printed in the Tombstone newspaper, the *Daily Epitaph*, a few days after the gunfight. The article gives information about the court hearing that was about to begin.